After the Tornado

After the Tornado

poems by

Diane Hueter

STEPHEN F. AUSTIN STATE UNIVERSITY PRESS
NACOGDOCHES ★ TEXAS

LIBRARY OF CONGRESS IN PUBLICATION DATA
Hueter, Diane
    After the Tornado / Diane Hueter
    ISBN: 978-1-62288-009-6

Book design: Laura Davis
Cover Art: *The Shed* by Ellen Vieth

Manufactured in the United States of America

Stephen F. Austin State University Press
P.O. Box 13007 SFA Station
Nacogdoches, TX 75962
sfasu.edu/sfapress
sfapress@sfasu.edu

Distributed by Texas A&M University Consortium
www.tamupress.com

Acknowledgments:

Grateful acknowledgment is made to the editors and readers of the following publications, in which poems in this collection have previously appeared:

Amarillo Bay: "Witnessing"
Amoskeag: "Facing the Storm"
Blueline: "Thanksgiving Cactus"
Borderlands: Texas Poetry Review: "After the Tornado," "Meteor Shower," "Communion"
Clackamas Literary Review: "Icicles"
Comstock Review: "For My Son, On His Birthday"
Concho River Review: "Following Krill"
Cottonwood Review Special Issue: "Drought," "Lilacs," "Lullaby," "Spring," "When My Grandfather Was a Logger"
DeKalb Literary Arts Journal: "For Donn"
Ellensburg Anthology "Watering Nasturtiums"
The Fourth River: "Nocturne"
Iowa Woman: "Chimney Swifts," "Drought," "Voices"
Iris: "August Conversation," "Digging Clams at Sequim Bay"
Iron Horse Literary Review: "Evening Song"
Isotope: "Dreaming After the Tornado"
KQ: "At Nine," "First Thunderstorm," "Josie's Tooth," "Sneaky Poem"
Pinyon: "In Memoriam: For Marjorie and Doris Lenore"
Platte Valley Review: "She Stops on the Stairs and Looks Out the Window"
PMS: Poem Memoir Story: "Self Portrait #7"
Spring Rain: "Nana's Music Box"
Tellus: "Greedy Season," "Vinland Valley"
Texas Review: "Childhood in the Drought"

Three Rivers Poetry Journal: "For a Girl Holding Eggs With Her Eyes Closed."

"Sweeping" and "Meteor Shower" appeared in *Times of Sorrow/ Times of Grace*, ed. by Saiser, Kosmicki, Sandlin. Omaha, Neb.: Backwaters Press, 2002. "In the Nest" appeared in *Texas Poetry Calendar 2001*, Flying Cow Productions, Fall 2000. "December 1," "Journeys" and "In the Nest" appeared in *In the Middle: Midwestern Women Poets*, ed. by Sylvia Griffith Wheeler. Kansas City, MO: BkMk Press, 1985. "When My Grandfather Was a Logger," "Nana's Music Box," "Lilacs," "Journeys," "December 1," and "In the Nest" appeared in *Kansas: Just Before Sleep*, by Diane Hueter. Chapbook, Cottonwood Review Press, 1978. "Communion" is displayed in the Blanton Museum of Art (Austin, Texas) alongside the painting "From That Day On" by Ben Shahn.

Some of these poems were first printed in slightly different forms.

Contents

In Memoriam: For Marjorie and Doris Lenore ❧ 13

Communion ❧ 15

Sisters ❧ 17

Nana Sends Me to My Room ❧ 20

Thanksgiving Cactus ❧ 21

Fighting ❧ 23

Witnessing ❧ 25

Nana: A Portrait Past All Understanding ❧ 26

Nana's Music Box ❧ 29

Lilacs ❧ 30

Facing the Storm ❧ 31

For Donn ❧ 32

Josie's Tooth ❧ 34

Digging Clams at Sequim Bay ❧ 35

Voices ❧ 38

My Father Feeds the Hummingbirds ❧ 41

At Nine ❧ 43

Chimney Swifts ❧ 44

Sneaky Poem ❧ 46

Meteor Shower ❧ 47

Following Krill ❧ 49

Sweeping ❧ 50

Nocturne ❧ 52

Stopping at My Grandmother's House ❧ 54

When My Grandfather Was a Logger ❧ 55

After the Tornado ❧ 56

Dreaming After the Tornado ❧ 57

First Thunderstorm ❧ 58

Evening Song ❧ 59

Spring ❧ 60

For My Son, On His Birthday ❧ 62

Childhood in the Drought ❧ 64

Drought ❧ 66

Watering Nasturtiums ❧ 67

In the Nest ❧ 68

For a Girl Holding Eggs with Her Eyes Closed ❧ 69

Vinland Valley ❧ 71

My Thanksgiving Cactus Blooms ❧ 72

In the Winter Garden ❧ 73

Traveling Home ❧ 74

Lullaby ❧ 75

Journeys ❧ 76

Icicles ❧ 77

Winter ❧ 79

December 1 ❧ 80

Greedy Season ❧ 81

Possum ❧ 82

She Stops On the Stairs and Looks Out the Window ❧ 83

Self Portrait #7 ❧ 86

About the Author ❧ 89

For Donn

In Memoriam: For Marjorie and Doris Lenore

Marjorie, she stepped off the school bus, right here
in front of the house. . . That last year, Doris Lenore was
just tired all the time . . .

Nana shows me where they dance,
the wee ones, beneath the maple tree.
Their bare feet, white as clover,
follow music we never hear.
When we dream in our cottony beds,
when the milk cows, if we had them,
would be locked asleep in the barn,
when the road stretches to the hilltop
like a black and icy river,
they gather here, prancing with mice and moles,
dressed in raspberry hats and columbine frocks,
prancing fairy rings beneath the tree.
That's all that ordinary folk will see.

I'm old enough to believe this, or not, if I choose—
I've overheard the other stories,
sitting like a teacup on the floor.
I've rummaged through the closets and uncovered
mice-nibbled copybooks and ribbons in tissued boxes.
I've found speckled feathers of fledgling robins
scattered across the lawn.

Nana turns, flaps her apron
at a cross-eyed cat, shoos it from the yard.
She cautions me and I know
to hold my breath past graveyards, toss salt
over my shoulder, keep a wary eye on wandering horses

slogging through the ditches up Pontius Road.

Schooled in hop and skip, in promenade and do-se-do,
this morning I kick off my raggedy slippers
to dance barefoot in damp grass, toadstools and clover.
Past the lilac, round the roses, I leap and twirl
as finely and fiercely as I can.
As if this morning could be forever,
I dance for Nana, coming to her side,
her joyful heathen, her little banshee,
the one who twirls and leaps
to make her sky sing welcome,
cloudless and blue.

Communion

based on the painting *From That Day On,* by Ben Shahn

1.

From that day on
he dreamt of swimming
in the falling snow.

He felt tiny minnows
nuzzling his legs
while snowflakes
fell on his shoulders.

He caught them on his tongue,
like a child playing in a meadow
not too far from home.

2.

From that day on
he dreamt of his wife
searching the fog-cradled beach
for oysters and mussels,
a fine meal for them all.

She holds a shadow
in her hands.
It shines like a pearl
not yet dried
by the heat of her skin.

3.

From that day on he dreamt
of the child lifted in his arms.

Hold her to the sky,
her eyes brown as butter clams,
what does she see?

Put the shell to her ear,
her smile and coo.
What does she hear?
How does she reply?

4.

From that day on he dreamt
he saw the thin paper of his life
scrolling away from him
across the whitecaps.

The fishing boat disappears.
The sun rises from the sea
like a dragon's gaping maw.

Snow falling still
from that day on.

Sisters

for my family

1. Marie

Marie, my companion,
decorated my breakfast spoon,
imprinted my skinny fist
with her polka-dot dress
and softly bobbed hair.

I thought she was my mother's sister,
gone before she entered first grade,
before my mother was even born,
family we'd lost when Nana was slim and smiling.

Oatmeal, cream of wheat, corn-flakes
mixed with tarnished silver;
every morning this ghostly tang sparked
my childish tongue.

Didn't everyone honor
the dead this way? Didn't all families
embellish the silverware?
Cherish chubby-cheeked girls
on silver-plated spoons?

2. Emilie

One morning in the china hutch drawer,
where embroidered napkins and tatted tablecloths
bumped up to the cribbage board

and the rubber-banded decks of cards,
I found another spoon, another sister.
Emilie, standing slightly turned,
but the same polka-dot dress,
bobbed hair, soft bubbly bow, her name spelled down
the spoon's narrow handle.
Emilie, with tarnished cheeks,
too scratched, too dented,
to come to the table.

3. Annette

Nana dealt a hand of cribbage or pinochle,
answered my eyes,
recounted for our neighbor—
her partner or opponent— the green stamp prize,
the cereal box award, celebrity children, Dionne quints.
We have more spoons somewhere, she said,
but not all five.

4. Yvonne

O Marie, my steady, my faithful
mealtime companion.
O Emilie, the hidden one.
I seek three more
whose names I'm not sure I know.
There are questions no one answers.
There are feasts no one enjoys.
Some are never called to the table.
O how skinny, how frail
they become.

5. Cecile

I have them all now.
Flushed out like tiny birds
from antique stores, garages, junk drawers:
one holds the hem of her dress in each hand, as if preparing to curtsey;
one keeps her hands behind her back, expecting no gifts;
one is so blackened and dented she seems angry, always unacknowledged;
one seeks the grace of God; one the soft pillow of a winter snowbank.
The smiles engraved on their faces
have not altered for many years.

Annette, Yvonne, Cecile, Emilie, Marie,
to each I say: "Hello, dear one,
I've found you."
The family gathers for breakfast again.
With the hunger of my young heart,
the hunger of my warm blood,
the hunger of my forgetting, my loss—
you are not truly mine, yet I claim you,
as hungry now as I have ever been.

Nana Sends Me to My Room

No, I didn't use the ladder
I climbed the fence
I leapt like a bird
clinging to the bark
I wasn't going to fall down
and get a cast like Jimmy
Janet didn't need to come
stand there crying in the ditch
The neighbors didn't say she
could eat their cherries
I can't sit under the roses all day
playing with the baby
Janet can, you bet, but not me
I don't believe the fairies dance there
It's damp and the grass stains my socks
No, I don't know where you found them
Yes, I'm going
to my room now
I hear you
Why don't you just
give me to the gypsies
next time they come by?
They'd let me dance barefoot in the grass
I'd have ribbons and curly hair
ride a white pony
eat sweet Bing cherries
from every tree I find

Thanksgiving Cactus

Nana's flowering cactus
perched on her kitchen windowsill
like a spiny green crab in tide pool shadows,
rooted and wary.

It seems Nana paid it no mind,
no more than she did her speckled hen,
scratching and pecking in the dusty yard,
flapping frantically away
whenever we ran pell-mell
through the house, slamming
the kitchen door, scattering
around the garage like hornets.

But perhaps she tended this cactus,
her unruly pet, carefully prodding
the potting soil, testing for proper moisture—
Too wet? Too dry? Will it rot
if watered now? I seem to see her bent
over the waving green branches,
squint-eyed, her hair tangled in pink curlers,
as if scolding a favorite child caught spooning
and spooning sugar into her tea.

Sometimes, when we were early
for breakfast, we'd find her
at the kitchen table,
as if she'd sat there all night.
She'd put a cooling palm
on our foreheads, smoothing our damp,

sleep-sweaty curls. We entrusted ourselves
to her cataract-clouded eyes.
Yes, surely, we bloomed before her—
her wild, improbable flowers.

Fighting

Grandpa called his cat Dempsey
after the boxer. I don't know
where he got it, and I don't care.
No one needs
to call me up and help me
remember. This is not
a genealogy
I'm reciting.

Grandpa called us little
pet names,
little pet names.
We were his timid
tiny mice.

Some mornings he made pancakes
with syrup and honey.
Dempsey got saucers of cream.
When Grandpa smiled at him,
that cat smiled back.

Grandpa had a cat then
and he called it Dempsey.
It caught mice in the kitchen
better than a trap

I don't know anything
about boxing, sparring and jabbing.
I can't remember any champions,
any heroes, just the name of his cat,

but I know he wasn't really our grandpa,
not yours, not mine—
he was her second husband
and no kin to us.

Tonight in another kitchen,
the table festive with candles and pine,
you chop potatoes, the knife
whacking the cutting
board. I pound stubborn jars on the counter,
to pry off the lids. Together
we tell our children
dinner will be ready soon.

But there is a timeless
circling in the ring: You say forgive
and forget? No. You say forget
and forgive? No. You say
some mighty hand
pulls the rope, the bell
clangs, and it's all over?
You tell me hating
is a sin, you tell me
I'm filled with bile, nothing I taste
will bring me joy. I only ask you
to remember, to imagine—
if our real grandfather had lived?
if that one hadn't
kept cats, hadn't craved mice?

Witnessing

Tugging on her sleeve and whispering
I tell Nana the neighbor's barn is on fire.
I've just seen the sheltering pines and cedars
explode into flame and orange-gold sparks scatter
from the roofline like children playing tag
or birds in the cornfield frightened by gunfire.

I feel myself become a faint companion
to the fire's bright and pulsing core.
Flowing from branch to branch,
relentlessly spiraling, something is escaping
from my trusting heart.
Stunned by the splendor, stunned
by the dark heaven, this impetuous flash
of pheasant wings
flying east and west
north and south
leaving nothing to anchor
the timid candle behind my eyes.

Nana: A Portrait Past All Understanding

When my Uncle Jack got divorced,
Nana ripped his wedding portrait in two,
severing his freckled and smiling wife
and dropping her into the cooking-stove fire.
I recognize that drama, that maternal demonstration.
It is something I might do, stone-eyed
above the fire's incandescent flash and crackle.

Some nights I picture Nana by the stove,
asking Grandpa to approve the turkey or the roast,
both of them beaming, the center of this family
ceremony, like a Norman Rockwell
Thanksgiving dinner; dishes waiting on the table,
windows steamed, children pulling off sweaters
and sitting expectantly, with skinny necks and arms
like hungry speckled robins.

Like a silent movie—
the men standing in the background
smoking cigarettes, sipping beer,
while my mother slips biscuits from the baking sheet
and Aunt Rick adds butter to the mashed potatoes.
There's Uncle Jack, my Nana's only son,
lanky and good humored, lounging
in a shadowy corner, grinning his crooked grin;
light flashes from his eyeglasses as he tilts
back in his chair.   There's Nana,
in her floral, rick-rack trimmed apron,
lifting the round cast-iron lid from the stove's firebox,
holding the slim sepia figure above the flames.

Maybe he cheers her,
startling the children with hearty, house-bursting laughter.
Or maybe it wasn't like that, maybe Nana was alone
and it was dark and the house was quiet and maybe—
(or maybe they were dead already—Uncle Jack,
my mother, the man who wasn't truly my grandpa—
all in the same cemetery, but not together.) Maybe
we were living in California then, in Los Angeles,
and she had no celebration, no children around her
circling like cheerful and adoring moons.
Maybe everyone stayed home,
drinking alone with only the blue television glow
and the cold stove and the warmth only of whiskey.
Maybe that's when she ripped the happy nuptial portrait
so my uncle's hand grasped only a disembodied elbow
as he stood, full of promise in his good suit and his boyish, rakish grin—
(oh, Jack, she once said to my brother, *he pissed his life away,*
drank it all and pissed it all away.)

Such an album of narrative possibilities—
such unbearable sadness— I remember the portrait whole,
displayed on Nana's upright piano, my Aunt Carol with hair so red
it flared even in the photo's monotone.
And I turn over and over in my mind,
like cards dealt in solitaire, those other photos,
stored in a box in my aunt's spare bedroom:
Nana's own portraits my aunt showed me
last time I was home, remarking on the damage, the flaws—
Nana, as a child, standing straight-bang solemn by her parents,
Nana, Babe and Hattie, smiling sisters with bobbed hair,
    climbing Mt. Si,
even snapshots I took of her holding my baby girls,
where she smiles quizzically to someone— I hope it is my mother—

standing behind me. I ask each image as it turns and slides into place,
When? When did she hold in her soft and creamy arthritic hands
that ordinary lead pencil and x out, cross out her face?
Each and every one?
What cracks? What fissures? What aches made sparks fly
as if her bones were dry twigs catching fire?

Nana's Music Box

Nana, soft as old quilts,
sweet as lilacs, pats cream
colored powder on her cheeks and chin.
Her music box plays a tune I can't remember.
Her mirror is covered with pictures of my kin.

Nana, soft as old quilts,
sweet as lilacs in spring,
I wish today were not September
in Kansas. To be small
and barely able to see my head in your mirror
between all the strange faces of my distant kin.
To be small and playing at your feet
with your blue music box
filled with powder as sweet as lilacs.

Nana, a tune I can't recall
rambles through my head. A string
of notes, a scale of dreams,
all jangled, misplaced, with a mistimed beat.
Something aches to cheat the years
as every year winds down. Something aches
to warm the earth, force the lilacs into bloom,
lift the lid, hear the tune.
Know the music before it breaks.

Lilacs

You should pick the flowers as they wither.
They will be like wrinkled skin between your fingers.
Strong, supple, but so near death your fingers touch the other world.
Drop them on the ground near the base of the bush.
If it rains they will melt beneath the mud.
If not they will dry up like dead insects.
Maybe the wind blows them away.

Facing the Storm

Beyond the porch light, Daddy sat in a deck chair
by the swimming pool, lighting his cigarette
in a momentary calm. He had a clear view
of the western sky, where thunderclouds roiled
like serpents of the deep and bolts of glory
shattered the heavens. Slender firs
swayed, wind-lashed supplicants in silhouette.

Our mother, she always stood
where she could see the red glow of his cigarette
out the square, uncurtained window.
Her fear of snakes, steep roadside chasms,
lightning and thunder, legendary among us.
Our bones told us she only played at ignoring him
as she swished soapy water around our dinner plates.

We knew so little then, we knew so much.
In nightgowns and pajamas,
our faces pressed to the patio door
we whispered our *oohs* and *ahs*. We counted
as they taught us—
one Mississippi two Mississippi—
and cherished them, steadfast and grounded
beneath the dazzle and flash burning across the sky.

For Donn

Last spring at nesting time
you hung strands of red yarn in the trees
where orioles and sparrows
grabbed it for their nests

Each time the wind blew
we could see the nests
hanging like baskets from high trailing branches

Now grey sky hangs down around the neighborhood
grey birds come to feed, crack seeds
and dart away
sour books glare down from the shelves

Stubble fields surround us
hawks sit broody on power poles

Days move by without shadows

I would burrow into my own skin
a mouse in my skull
without even stars to light my cave
but somehow the bright yarn
in bare trees
reads like your name
smells like your hair
and though I still cannot feel the pregnant
load of summer
I almost see our children
swinging through the air

arms and legs brown
flashing like small birds among dense leaves

Dancing and singing
you anchor me down

Josie's Tooth

petal of ivory
    hanging

already
    the color is different
from her other teeth

more blue
    more shadows

not here   not gone

Digging Clams at Sequim Bay

Pine trees lean precariously over the cliff
Thrust roots in all directions
Red as rust
Like the long crooked legs of crabs.

The tide, finished receding,
Turns to retrace the cycle
And my brother digs under water
Wet and sand-plastered past his knees
All the way up the sleeves of his shirt.

We've overslept
But he will not have us miss a moment
Of this day.
The foggy sky hangs like dawn for hours
And gulls wander aimlessly
Under fog-shrouded trees.

Dogs dash into the water
after sticks or ropes of kelp
my brother's children toss.

They are so quick they seem to prance
A moment on top of the water
Before they sink
Belly deep and cold.

* * *

Did I stand there with Josie

Balanced on my hip?
Or was it Erin, years later?
Someone whimpered over the cold
The sand
The wind

I watched the houses across the iron bay
To see if anyone came out
Paused at the shore
Or got in a boat to chug away.
No one did.

Through the light fog
The houses, red and white toys,
Lay scattered along the bank.
I waited for the fisherman
Or his wife
To stand waving from the headland
A miniature lighthouse
A beacon to the farther shore.

      * * *

Every year I left the plains behind
And took my daughters home
As if there were charms to turn their blood
To sea water.

Barnacles, mussels, kelp.
It was my litany.

My mother would hold them,
Or take snapshots for her album,

Or wander up the beach
Fitting small pebbles
Into the palms of their hands,
Filling their pockets
With sea glass and agates.

      *   *   *

It must have been the summer we felt
Death hovering in the fog.
Did the shovels clang ominously
Against hidden boulders?
Did the clams emerge broken open and limp
Pale suckers hanging from our hands?
Which damn child whispers into the sleeve of my coat
I'm cold, I'm cold, I'm cold?

Voices

1.

My mother sits by the window
with a cup of coffee and a crossword puzzle,
her hair in small pink rollers.
She rubs her eyes and takes another sip.

She does not think of the French word
for summer, Spanish gold or Scarlett's home,
fossil found in Java.
The patterned squares
and darkened corners
surround her like a quilt,
but give no warmth.

2.

She hides beneath a new scarf
so her own mother will not see
the gradual loss of hair.
Beneath her blouse
little x's on her chest
to align the radiation machine
and a mark on her calendar
for the next session of chemotherapy.

If she spoke to the mirror
her words would be
strong

and *bitter.*

She would say
secrets, secrets, secrets
and we would all nod
as if we understood.

3.

Dear Mom,
we are fine
how are you

Dear Mom
we are fine

Dear Mom
listen

Before they turn out the lights
Josie reads a bit from Black Beauty
Erin's high voice
neighs along from under the covers

Enchanted
silky black as that proud stallion
your granddaughters race and race
across the prairie
masked in brightness

4.

I sit on the back step
holding the early morning sun
in my cup of coffee
The cellar's aluminum door
slants into the hillside
a perch for cats as they wait for meals
a measure of rain on cloudy days

I think of canning and saving
boiling
strawberry jam
I think of hibernating
sleeping long
singing in the roots of trees

5.

I hear them at work
at my desk
at night making love
in the morning when I pour cornflakes
into bowls for breakfast
I hear them in the white milk
falling limply from the carton

I brush her hair
I braid it
I hear them as my fingers work back and forth
criss-cross methodically
every blond wisp
that strays from the strand

My Father Feeds the Hummingbirds

We both see it darting from the shade of the great cedar,
rushing up the ridge of the holly hedge,
swirling around the empty feeder.
"There's a hummer," my father says, "the first one this year."
He fumbles for a spoon in the drawer,
stirs the sugary concoction with hands I've just seen
cradling his coffee cup, gnarled and veined,
but no longer black with grease, bruised
with the purple nails of labor.
I watch him cross the yard,
trailing his oxygen tank and tube.
He stretches to the empty feeder,
taking it down, filling it,
each step carefully weighed,
measured by aching joints,
by lungs that struggle to inhale, exhale.
He turns, sees me
through the window and
                      I see him,
my task-master, my hurraher, my judge,
in each day of his days yet to come—
noon or dusk or chilly morning—
hoisting the pink-nectar lamp, the rosy lantern,
reaching for the hook on the pine tree.
I see him surrounded by hosts of shimmering birds,
emerald and sapphire wings purring, circling
his up-raised arm, his balding head
like ballerinas gathering for a twirling dance.
I realize then, or hope, he suddenly
one day understood the practicality of feathers

and the deep well of grace
within his own frame.

At Nine

I climbed to the top of the cedar.
Wet spring and all the branches
Soft on my arms and cheek. For hours
The sky as blue
As nothing on my mind.

Chimney Swifts

We sit together at dusk, before bed.
Her hair, pale and wispy
as the moon behind the elm,
glows, a faint lantern at my shoulder.

Chimney swifts flash across the sky,
chasing mosquitoes and gnats,
dipping down to drink from the pond.
They soar above our heads
and she points to them as they cross
the dark silhouette of our home.

Her lisping, toothless voice rises
as she tells me of the young birds cheeping
in the chimney of her room.
She listens as she paints at her easel,
as she plays jacks on the floor,
at night as she falls slowly to sleep
in her hot, sticky bed.
She listens for the beat of strong wings
fanning the chimney shaft
and the hungry babies' clamor.

Though all I see now are fireflies
in the long grass by the gate,
I know her eyes are bright as pebbles,
blue as dragonflies she hunts in the garden.
I know her heart is fertile as kernels of corn
and fresh as squash blossoms in the morning.
I know her eyes are tired and heavy

and she will soon nod at my side.
The long days of August stretch before us yet.
Nights of near silence,
only the sound of the combine moving slowly
back and forth across the hill.
Come autumn, we will clean the chimney for winter fires.
Each year a harvest of small bodies
barely feathered
eyes slate-colored behind translucent lids.

Sneaky Poem

I doubt that children really
come from lilacs and wine
more likely it was the musty moon
above the chicken coop
and some funky rock and roll on the radio

They whisper wetly in my ear
a quick secret
"just a minute, I have to go to the bathroom"

Meteor Shower

Lying by your side in the convent orchard,
in the unmown midnight lawn,
I turned to tell you I felt the dew
settling on my face and folded hands,
smelled sweet pears and apples
each time the breeze stilled,
their bouquet covering us like rain.

I could have been a stone
resting on a murky lake bottom,
when our child rolled like a minnow
beneath my skin
like a sudden silent galaxy.

Streaks of light sparkled
behind broken cloud;
there, and there.
Together our hands floated—
white moths among the branches—
while somewhere around us
a soul stood in awe of itself,
waiting to be found.

As we walked home,
we filled our pockets with purple plums,
small yellow pears and apples.
We didn't know she would be slow to talk,
but one day say "A is for avalanche"
and almost never stop. We didn't know
she would chant, "My daddy

is a hexagon, my momma is a diamond"
as she mounted the stairs to nap.
We saw only the light from our kitchen window,
the cat sitting by the table,
the bowl waiting for fruit.

Following Krill

We've been talking since I arrived,
sitting at the picture window
overlooking the Sound.
The sky is getting darker,
but we haven't yet admitted
that we were ever lost.

I watch the tide shifting,
ribbon-streaked, and when I decipher
what I see there, I show my father a spouting whale.

Through binoculars, hump
and flukes roll into the light, shining
black as briny water silvers down.

My father says sometimes at high tide
he hears them blasting as they swim
close to the cliff. He wonders if they've ranged
too far off course, following krill
into the Strait, then down to the Sound.
They are too big for this small water, and maybe—
my father never finishes telling me
the story of his life.

Sweeping

The girls tell me of a treasure,
and though their hands are empty
now, they want it.
Please, Momma, please,
a snake skin, Momma,
by the garden fence
all in one piece
and it rustles
when we touch it.
Does it sound like paper?
Like book leaves turning
when we read a story?
Or is it like little voices?
Does it rustle like little voices?
Like a child sleeping
warm under the quilts?
My questions won't
stop them.
They know my fear
of snakes. Teasing, they giggle
and squirm. Their boots
leave swirls of mud
on worn linoleum. I
tell them
it makes no difference,
this house holds so much dust,
so many shadows and dreams. Surely
one more will fit.
But if I
could stretch my hands

to the ceiling, crack my skin
along my spine, coil
and uncoil,
slither free along
the baseboards
toward the door,
Would I?
Would I?
Long ago?
What keeps me here
sweeping farmhouse dust
from room to room?
The moon above the chicken coop?
The calf waiting by the fence?
The little voices from upstairs?
The silence?

Nocturne

The back gate bangs
each time the wind changes,
unhinging me from sleep.
Then I hear his breath
unfettered and dreamy
beside me.

                Someday
he will be gone
or you will. Then everything
will be gone, no matter what.

No, even in darkness
I remember counting meteors
the fire-ripped sky opening before us
like some holy dream—
it will last forever.

                Forever, really?
if you had known then—
if you had seen—
you would have stopped
you wouldn't have had the strength
to take one step.

No, ours was a simple journey,
the burdens, the obligations
slid so smoothly around our borders
like breezes across closed eyes—

Then let yourselves fly
like a pair of migrating birds.
Let yourselves fly beneath a cloudless turquoise sky—
and, because the years are heavy,
take turns being the wind—

Stopping at My Grandmother's House

I see my father's truck, so I stop in,
the steepest hill to home is just beyond,
and Grandma doesn't like me to hike it in the dark.

Daddy smokes too much to catch the stench on me,
and neither one can tell when a teen-ager's stoned,
so I sit with gingersnaps and tea, listening to them talk.

Grandma's sure the cedar's grown too big,
its thrusting roots buckle the basement wall.
My father says, *Dry rot, someday*

the whole house will tumble in.
The lawn needs mowing, I'll send Jim
or Tom tomorrow. Dade, you done?

Before we leave, Daddy takes out the trash,
Grandma and I fill a flat of raspberries,
wrap red and yellow dahlias in a newspaper cone.

There's even rhubarb for a pie
I will bake. Daddy's truck will be warm,
we'll listen to the radio news,

maybe it will sprinkle, the windshield wipers
waving back at us. Another bus rumbles
up Ballinger Way, but I have my ride home.

When My Grandfather Was A Logger

These things I remember:
huckleberries,
hot roads of red dust,
young trees crowding the road so close
they scraped both sides of the car
each time we passed
bumping slowly over clumps of grass and wild flowers.
And the dust itself covering everything.
The trees I can name:
red cedars and maples
pine trees with spring's new growth a pale lime-green
at the tip of each branch.
The trees themselves
haloed by dust and sun.

These too:
rusty iron cables,
the big Cat, the chain saw,
the way it always coughed into silence
and how we all stood
poised on the earth
like trees.
The moment our souls grew branches
and tottered,
we hesitated before a high breeze.

After the Tornado

After she saw the tornado splinter the hackberry trees
standing at field's edge; after she saw the hymnals
and purple velvet cushions of Coal Creek Gospel Hall
rise up and twirl like hellish dancers in cobra's trance;
and after she witnessed the tornado itself
diminish and sink back into the black cloud ceiling,
exhaling pews and tree limbs like candy wrappers from a passing car,
only then, after all, could she return
to her body and her breath, like a bird
unborn, returning to the shell. She could take up
her storm-stopped chores: straightening
the swing set's tangled chains,
gathering sun-dried sheets from the line,
feeding the caged rabbit a few blades of grass.

She could feel her fear-struck heart rolling in her chest
like grackles swarming in the yard and rising from the elm.

Because she could not gather the girls and their father
like a line of sun-warmed laundry tight in her arms,
she swept the floors clean as pearled barley, stood crayons
shoulder-to-shoulder in a bright sturdy box,
like irises framed by the kitchen window.

Dreaming After the Tornado

Even now, as she sleeps deeply in her quiet house
below windows thrown open to drought and grasshoppers,
she sees herself splintering like the scorched field's tossed fence posts,
her eyelids flutter—stripped leaves—

She searches the prairie for the path to follow
and the break in the mountains where she will gallop like a child
down the last steep slope to the salt water sound
where she was born. Home, she will watch her grandmother
pencil an almost indecipherable note to add
to the great-grandchild's birthday present.
She will sit with her parents as they read the evening news,
work the crossword puzzle. Beneath the fireplace painting
of boulders lashed by angry waves, she will hold up her hands,
gleaming wet, as she measures them against the spray.

She's leaving snakes in the kitchen, mice in the food,
leaving the silver cracked fence posts and silky-eyed hawks.
She knows she will always hear the midnight combines
rumble across darkened hills, piling up thunder and lightning,
twining her dreams together like golden straw in starry bales of hay.

First Thunderstorm

the flash caught her eye
like a light bulb shorting out
     much later   thunder

she opened the back door
and watched the dead bushes
by the apartments rock
back and forth in the wind
watched the water run down the street
carrying a wash of sand
filling the cul de sac drains

dark clouds rolled overhead
a few more raindrops fell

another flash of lightning
and faint thunder

and she remembered
she had no seeds planted
nothing sleeping
waiting to grow

quietly she closed the door
          past blocks and blocks of rooftops
          the fuzzy outline of budding trees

Evening Song

You open the window, catch
the sweet scent of flowers and hesitate—
nothing you see matches this fragrance,
no blooms captivate your eyes
the way the scent steps into your room
—a bed of yellow daffodils?
creamy poet's eye? purple hyacinth?
No, not these, wilted, wind tattered
and bent, not the maple, though suddenly
leafy, and not the petal-barren cherry
where the mockingbirds nest.
Yet listen, they sing, this ancient choir,
and lifting up, show you how to take
some gladness from the breeze.

Spring

1. March

The toad hunkers down again
backing into his burrow
beneath the sharp dry spikes
of last summer's spearmint.
His clammy grey hide the color of cold earth
dark spots like eyes all down his back.
She calls the others to come look.
One greets him like a tiny storybook friend.
The other asks: "Where? Where?
I don't see anything?"

2. April

The clothesline sags with duty
legs of jeans flap in the wind.
Shirts open unbuttoned
and billow out in welcome.
Her mouth fills with the taste
of her own children's hair.
Just washed or sweaty and dirty
it is the same joy.

When the clothes dry
she unclips them
and drops them into the basket
shirts socks jeans
they tumble together like lovers at night.

One child stirs with restless dreams
awakens suddenly to say
please oh please
let me
a little longer
She asks: What? What?
and must turn back the covers
to straighten the small body in bed.

3. May

What is the language they speak now on the rim?
my eyes do not see
my nose does not smell
my ears do not hear
through the soles of my feet
the hollow of my bones
the pit of my womb
I feel the quake, the torrent

4. June

She checks the sky and the clothesline
charms herself to sleep
in her dreams
they eat the yellow bulbs
the yellow flowers
nickels and pennies and dimes
as if they swallowed them whole
to be richer and richer

For My Son, On His Birthday

I know little of sons, only that he is my other child—
not daughter, not sister—my third child, fabulous
son of my wandering.
                                          I might tell him
my favorite story, how early one morning,
the sun still low below long banks of black firs,
I row this fledgling, my fluffy headed son, across the lake.
The lake only wavers where the oars touch,
currents rippling from the rowboat's prow
as it glides like a trout through water black and still.

"I am three," my son says, reaching over
to trail his fingers in the lake.
"No," I reply, quitting my steady strokes,
holding the oars so they drip
beads of water, waiting for reflections
to settle. "Today is your birthday. Today you are four."
He laughs, because he knows he didn't change
overnight, my still unhatched chickadee,
my unbruised cherry plum.

A bald eagle perches on the topmost branch
of a lightning-struck tree. I want to tell him,
my son, "Turn and look," teach him the word
of soaring, of flight, teach him the bird's name.
I want to counter the depth of the black
mirror poised beneath the oars.

My son shivers, but he wants to swim
and I let him. While he floats in black

cold water, arms spread, fingers
fanned, his lips turning faintly blue,
I tell myself he's safe, I'm here. He floats
on his back, a water skimmer, pale and Christ-like,
his thin limbs like saplings stripped of bark.
Then this child I do not speak of,
child of my slumbering mind, floating
like a fingerling in morning's half-light,
shuts his eyes, smooth as water-worn stones
found in a kitchen drawer. My magnet, my
chickadee, he will not cry. My cherry plum, faithful
son of my reckless wandering, lodestar, he does not
cry and I too am silent as I pick up the oars, take sight
of true north, perhaps for the last time, and row back to shore.

Childhood in the Drought

Beneath the spring-blooming spirea,
The green and white phantom by their porch,
The girls scratch tiny words and their own short names
In petalled dust.

"Good-bye," they say, "Good-bye,"
Sweeping themselves away with their hands.

The sky fades to rags behind the chicken coop.
Brown fields seem streaked by careless mopping.
The trees empty themselves like leaking buckets
Spilling dried leaves over the husks of cicadas and grasshoppers.

In the house, Momma sings with a mouthful of stones.
Daddy's eyes flake like chips from granite.

Where are the summer marigolds
Tiger-eyed blossoms with frilly emerald leaves?
Where are the zinnia rows
Jasper bowls
Holding the clouds' sweet breath
Glowing in the dusk like starlight's river?

Momma sings with a mouthful of stones.
Daddy's eyes crack like splinters from quartz.

The girls throw pebbles through chicken wire,
Making the resting hens cluck softly
And rustle in the dust.
They tie a rope to the fence pole,

So one can turn and the other hop.
They chant so quietly no one hears—
Moonstone, agate, opal, pearl—
Remembering a time when everyone laughed
And light poured out the open window.

Drought

An impulse took her by the lake
instead of down the highway
directly home

Among the trees
the sky fell like cotton

And where one winter they had skipped stones
clanging and echoing across solid ice
now mud-caked fence posts trace
the faint ruts of a driveway

"It's a sweet dream," sang the radio
the water so low she could see
the farm house foundation
the cistern's cement lid
and corroded handle
shingles scattered like doll clothes

She could point to where she knew
the lilacs should stand
and the elm tree with the swing
         She knows
there was never a promise made here
that was not broken

Watering Nasturtiums

two houses down
May hangs her wash on the line
listening to the first inning

birds spool out slow songs
from the branches
of summer stung trees

the rusty pump squeaks
water gushes into the buckets
and splashes on my feet
as I trudge bent over
to the flower beds

May shouts, "Birds! Birds!"
and flaps a pillowcase
at the sky

the birds' song pours
like water from a bucket
pools on the caked earth
water on water now
all the sound we hear

In the Nest

we wake to this
sun in the sky
like a blow between the eyes

we dry soon
smashing the curves
of clouds
with our wings

our feathers
white
like milkweed fluff
your grandfather's hair
cottonwood bloom
on the naked river

born to the strength of long horizons
we never gamble
we need no alibis

all our stories begin this way
"such small bones
a rabbit has"

For a Girl Holding Eggs With Her Eyes Closed

1.

all my childhood I was a bee
I lived in sweetness
and apple blossoms
the sky was bright and warm
the trees my giant brothers

yesterday I forgot to water your plants
today crumbs dust the tablecloth
it's been years since I tried to dance
I'm not sure anymore
what to make of it all

and who shall I ask?
the girl holding eggs?
what does she see
standing that way?

2.

why do we stumble over words
each time we talk
even the story of the cricket
is more direct

3.

I would send you a letter of wine

a letter of straw
a letter of stone

this is my heart
these are my bones
this will hold my heart when I am dead

Vinland Valley

go on go on
what's next?
what happens next?
who rings the doorbell?
who answers the door?
who comes in and sits down by the fire?
who makes a pot of tea?
who drinks hot-buttered rum?
who knits? who crochets?
who sits with the cat in her lap?
who stares out the window?

nothing
nothing happens
no one rings the doorbell
no one answers the door
no one comes and sits down, feet up close to the fire
no one makes a pot of tea
no one's thirsty
no one knits or sews or darns
no one pets the cat
no one stares out the window
watching snow fall on the walkway

My Thanksgiving Cactus Blooms

Dragon hearts breaking open
tempting, predatory,
with flaming cinder-tipped tongues–
from these lips I learn
my midnight destiny, my fiery disguise.

In the Winter Garden

bulbs
chime like my heart

ring through leaf and loam
every note striking

smooth as bone
mole and shrew

hibernate beneath the hollyhocks
each has a home in the chorus

awake and sing with starry mouths
tunnel through the snow

track the rough brown parchment
that sheathes those sounding bells

we will hear the holy chant
the sacred harmony

Traveling Home

When the night shines like black beetle wings
When the cricket sings for luck
When I've taken myself out into the universe
I recall, as if it is my own memory,

Your story about one starry night
Traveling through Montana
Unlucky hitchhikers at midnight, husband and wife
Hiking down a high mountain road together

Though I only move from room to room
Sliding across the cold floors
Moving from window to window
Like a shaggy pony following a fence line

I remember again the things I treasure
Kneading dough in the warm kitchen
The moment the winter garden awakens
Saying yes when someone asks

Lullaby

we wake dreamless
mute
we brood in the dark corners of houses
we never light candles
as we did when we were young
and made love
to rock and roll music

tired and hollow as owls
we hoot and hoot
this night the moon is covered by snow clouds

I dream of mice
creeping up the sleeves of my nightgown
their cold noses
and damp paws in the white
hollow shell of my elbow
I cradle them as if they are my children
I cradle them as if I am ready to sing

Journeys

My hands swim away.
Across the lake
they nestle down and dream,
the mud holds them like a mother.

My toes
perch in the bare trees
like a flock of sparrows.
They taste the wind with each ruffled feather.
The ripe season is a promise in their throats.

My arms and legs have destinations they do not speak of.
They scurry across the road
disguised as dry oak leaves.
I'm sure she gathers them
and burns them in a pile.
They come home smelling of smoke
and do not talk for days.

Icicles

She stood in the chilled and darkened room
because the only telephone was in a room
shut off each year against the cold.
By the light, it was late afternoon.
Cold though, the trees were bare,
icicles hung from the gutters.

She held a blanket around her shoulders
as she listened to her father tell her
you had died.
Her father only calls when someone dies,
so it is no surprise.
And since her mother is already gone,
and her father is speaking,
it can't be too bad.
But it was the season they lost the pup to coyotes,
and the neighbor's dog slaughtered all their chickens
when they were at work.
The winter they marveled at water spilled from a jug.
The time it froze as it hit the cooking pot—
then froze in the jug, too.

So it was winter when she learned of your death.
Outside the window, icicles glittered
with the weak sun's last denial.
Trees opened their arms
so the birds could fly.
Maybe that's why it was all so clear for a moment—
the birds' bodies across the sky
like burnt images,

the road's snow-filled ruts,
the sun hanging onto that last tree on the horizon
like an icicle just before it drops and shatters—

She heard her husband and children in the back room
by the fire, laughing,
as her father tells her of your death.
He can't know so many
have waited for this news
as if they'd slept for years in winter's darkest room.
And he would be shocked to know
how many are glad—
for a moment, she was ready suddenly to say
as if it poured from her like water—

Good
Good I'm glad

But she stopped,
because it hurt so much she couldn't see.

Winter

The moon makes a long journey up the hill to our house,
across the valley and up the path,
illuminating the grassland's fragile geometry.

Stubble fields covered in snow,
deep shadows along windbreak trees,
each stalk and twig—
moonlight praises these sharpened distances.

I shiver and close my door against the gleam,
pull curtains across the windows,
poke the kitchen fire into flame.

I climb the stairs again
to cover the sleeping girls
with quilts and down-filled comforters.
The bedroom's wood-burning stove crackles,
the cat sleeps in the valley between two small still bodies,
her whiskers twitching as mice skitter in the closets
and phantom footsteps creak up the stairs.

Later, I climb the stiff branches of the bare oak tree,
rest where the hangman's noose left its burn.
It seems all night I will listen to her stories,
a child at her feet, beguiled, like the wind
twisting its way up the drafty stairwell,
remembering the dreams I've dreamt and left
hanging on barbs of frost-sparkled fence-wires.

December 1

I sit so close to the stove
my left leg bakes beneath my jeans
I could be dough
rising beneath a folded towel

outside the sun shines
frozen earth turns to mud
but the wind
coming from the northlands
forces open all the sealed cracks
in the weak joinings of our windows and doors

my leg burns
this close dry heat is bad for my boots
the joints of my fingers
like chicken claws
would make poor soup

the wind has come so far to tell me this

Greedy Season

I want to be fat
like squirrels and bears
my cheeks popping with nuts

I want to be fat
and sleek
rotund
wrapped in warmth

glutton
glutton
I will not sleep out the season
but will sit here
my feet propped against the stove
my shirt front greasy and stained
blisters on all ten
of my greasy fingers

Possum

slow man possum
eats eggs in the hen house
snotty nose and rat-like tail
Mama pokes him with a stick
saying go
slow man possum
go leave the hen house
and the eggs
find some slow man possum hole
far away
under a tree
or in a pile of scrub brush
where slow man possum
can be happy
with possum children
and possum wife
snow white rose red
hit the possum on the head
Mama's in the kitchen
baby's in the bed
Mama bakes a pan of good corn bread
Papa's in the garden
shovel in his hand
snow blood blossoms
slow man possum
move along
move along

She Stops On the Stairs and Looks
Out the Window

Because this icy stairwell
is lit only by a harsh bare bulb
dangling like fruit from the high ceiling . . .
Because this stairwell landing is over
3,000 miles from home and the voices
on the telephone and the news the telephone brings . . .
Because the wallpaper was lovingly chosen
and carefully hung maybe twenty,
maybe fifty years ago . . .

This is where the creaking house
still shows its age,
layers of wallpaper splayed open
like geological faults, russet colored,
powdery like flour,
large cracks in horsehair plaster
and places where plaster let go,
disintegrated, crumbled to dust,
wooden laths and two-by-fours
marked by faint carpenter pencil.
Because the past is unremarked
and unremarkable . . .
Because the high drafty passageway
leads from the tumult of life to the tumult
of slumber and dreams,
from the lopsided kitchen
to the cold painted bedrooms . . .

Because she stops as if sudden thought
or memory held her, hanging like the bare bulb
on a storm shattered branch . . .

The north wind rattles the frost-painted panes
almost enough to crack or break.
The frayed blanket
nailed to the stairwell bottom
flutters and billows, and the bedroom
door rocks on its hinges.
Because she knows aged men
breathed their last lonely breath
in rooms above her . . .
Because children tossed in fever . . .
Because worn calico and gingham women
left by the front door
disgraced and divorced and their living
children would never see the father
again, only receive enough money
annually for one pair of shoes . . .

She looks to the wolf-black sky,
seeing ice below her
and fire ahead and nothing to stop
the bone-cracking, tear-freezing gale
that shakes the window glass, spits
down the chimney, gallops like horses
through all the rooms, chilling her children,
girls intent with crayons,
surrounding their pointy houses,
their sun and grass and flowers,

nipping their stick-figure family
drawn all in a row, smiling hand-in-hand.
Because she cannot separate millet
from rice, cannot untangle
silk thread from sheep's wool, cannot
remember the name of the dwarf . . .
Because at dusk the day-thawed snow
begins to freeze again, slick-glazed paths
to the outhouse and well . . .

The fairytale always ends
with this row of footprints frozen in ice.

Self Portrait #7

I only wanted to paint myself riding my first bike,
its bright blue frame, silver handlebars,
sturdy black tires. For this occasion, I've taped
crepe paper streamers to the handle grips,
twined them in the spokes. No better way to celebrate
than gliding down a long hill, with your arms
thrown wide to the heavens.
But I've trapped myself completely
with this portrait in which I am speeding
like a crazy child, curled over silver
handlebars like a petal, furiously blooming.
Black asphalt flies behind me like a cape
and even the leaves of the maple trees,
turning yellow and red around the spokes of trunks,
radiate the frenetic energy of a hallucination.

That speck in the background, that blot
like a tiny fly stuck in oil, is the devil.
Like a wicked stepfather, he pretended to steady
the bike. You might not even notice him,
but he hunches over, grabbing his knees,
sucking in the dust of my wheels
with great gulps of his reddened and sweaty cheeks.
And because you can't see his eyes,
only the top of his balding head,
I paint crows on every bare branch.
They watch with great interest, great intent,
the pebbles that fly up from my tires.
I paint these pebbles with ivory and white—
some look like apple blossoms, some look like skulls,

some look so much like baby teeth
they should be pillowed in the clouds.

About the Author

DIANE HUETER'S poems have appeared in
*Comstock Review, Clackamas Literary Review, Texas
Review,* and *Borderlands: Texas Poetry Review.* She
reads poetry submissions for *Iron Horse Literary
Review* and lives in Lubbock, Texas, with her
husband. She works in the Southwest Collection/
Special Collections Library at Texas Tech University.

CPSIA information can be obtained
at www.ICGtesting.com
Printed in the USA
LVOW11s0637040418
572132LV00007B/756/P